What Do We Know About
Atlantis?

by Emma Carlson Berne

illustrated by Manuel Gutierrez

Penguin Workshop

For the students
of Wyoming Middle School—ECB

Per la mia perduta principessa atlantidea—MG

PENGUIN WORKSHOP
An imprint of Penguin Random House LLC, New York

First published in the United States of America by Penguin Workshop, an imprint of
Penguin Random House LLC, New York, 2022

Visit us online at penguinrandomhouse.com.

Library of Congress Cataloging-in-Publication Data is available.

Printed in the United States of America

ISBN 9780593386880 (paperback)   10 9 8 7 6 5 4 3 2 1 WOR
ISBN 9780593386897 (library binding)   10 9 8 7 6 5 4 3 2 1 WOR

Contents

What Do We Know About Atlantis?

The hot sun blazed down on Spyridon's head. He pulled his pith helmet farther down his brow and ignored the sweat trickling down his neck. He sat back on his heels and gazed into the excavated pit in front of him. Spyridon Marinatos had been an archeologist for forty years. By 1967, he was a professor. He was the inspector general of the Greek Antiquities Service. He'd excavated too many artifacts in his career to count. But this—*this*—was the most exciting dig he'd ever led.

They'd only been digging for a few weeks on the Greek Island of Santorini, but already, they'd found a stone doorway, the base of a column, and piles of old pottery. People had lived here—lots of people. Now, the forty miners helping the team were carefully scraping away the hard, chalky dirt.

Most of the nearby villagers were busy harvesting their tomato crop, but a few wandered away from their fields to watch. Then, a shout went up. One of the diggers had found flakes of plaster—white. Spyridon ran over to him. Frescoes!

The plaster was from painted murals that had once decorated the walls of ancient buildings and homes.

The excitement spread. The team kept digging. The artifacts were everywhere, all around them—more painted frescoes: black, pink, green, red. Walls reinforced by wooden poles, huge limestone blocks that must have supported giant buildings, cooking pots, wine jugs, looms for weaving, paved streets, plumbing systems! This ancient civilization had *running water*!

The weeks went by and the dig went on. More and more treasures were unearthed. There were huge murals of flowers, women, and bulls. One showed three ladies in a field full of crocus blossoms. Another showed a group of monkeys climbing rocks beside a river. The team found three-story buildings with elaborate staircases.

They found paved roads and huge storage rooms filled with containers of wine and oil. There were artifacts from other places in the world. These ancient people traveled, which meant they must have had ships. Somewhere under there, Spyridon suspected, there could be a palace.

An ancient city, full of beautiful art and graceful buildings. A wealthy city with many ships. A city and its people buried forever in a sudden explosion of molten lava and ash. An island vanished overnight.

Could this be *it*? The lost city of Atlantis?

No, Spyridon insisted. He was a professional scientist and a respected professor, not a storyteller. He was certain the story of Atlantis was a myth. It was only a legend, wasn't it?

CHAPTER 1
The Lost City

The story of Atlantis begins in about 360 BCE, during the time of the ancient Greeks. It is the story of a paradise described by a philosopher named Plato. The people in Plato's beautiful city were wealthy and powerful. But they weren't just people. They were half-god and half-human (called demigods). This place wasn't ruled by a president or a king. Instead, its ruler was Poseidon, the Greek god of the seas.

In this gorgeous city, flowers bloomed, tree branches waved in the sun, and fruit and grain of every type grew tall under the blue sky. Elephants wandered the land. People made jewelry and decorations from precious metals more valuable than gold. They had plenty of stone for building and carving.

The demigods controlled a vast fleet of ships. They traveled all over the world and brought back treasures to decorate their huge houses. They had hot and cold running water in their bathhouses. They had separate baths for men and women, and even for horses. They had paved streets and a massive racetrack for their horses.

And the people of this city were wealthy enough to build an elaborate temple to Poseidon at the center of town and decorate it with sheets of silver. They carved a massive sculpture of Poseidon standing in a chariot, with a hundred attendants riding dolphins around him. Walls of

gold surrounded the temple, along with golden statues.

These demigods were happy in their paradise. They lived peacefully among the green grass and blue waters. They were wise and calm and not concerned with money or power. They worshipped their gods and the gods protected them.

Greek Gods

The ancient Greek civilization worshipped a group of twelve gods and goddesses, led by Zeus, king and chief god, and his wife and queen, Hera. Each of the gods and goddesses ruled over different areas of human life. Athena was the goddess of wisdom and war. She was also Zeus's favorite daughter. Apollo was the god of music, archery, and healing. Poseidon, the sea god, created storms. Aphrodite was the goddess of beauty and love.

The Greek myths said that the gods and goddesses lived on top of Mount Olympus, the highest mountain in Greece. They married each other, fought each other, and had children together, just like humans. They watched over the lives of humans, and they could protect or punish them as they wished.

Zeus

Plato said that Atlantis was made up of islands lying inside each other in rings. Water separated these rings, and a canal ran right down the middle. This was so ships could sail through. The Atlanteans built their homes using colors of stone: black, white, and red. They decorated all the walls around their islands with brass and tin. Their ships floated in a huge port, and the island had a big, flat plain for growing crops.

The Atlanteans, Plato said, were perfect. Their life was perfect. Until it wasn't.

As the years went by, the Atlanteans started getting greedy. They started becoming more like people and less like gods. They grew selfish and forgot how to get along. They fought with one another, trying to snatch more and more wealth and power.

The gods were watching, of course, and they did *not* like what they were seeing. Zeus, the god

of the sky and the ruler of all gods and humans, declared that the Atlanteans needed to be punished. He'd take care of that. In one night, Zeus struck Atlantis down. He sent fire rolling over the city and earthquakes to shake apart the

land. Buildings tumbled into the sea. People were swept into the water. And the city of Atlantis, trembling and cracking, sank down, down, under the roiling waves, to the bottom of the sea, never to be seen again.

Plato (427 BCE–347 BCE)

The Greek philosopher Plato was actually named Aristocles. His wrestling coach started calling him Plato, which means "broad," possibly because of his big shoulders. He had two brothers and a sister. His family lived in Athens, Greece. They were wealthy and active in politics. Plato was probably expected to go into politics, too.

But when he was young, Plato enjoyed writing

plays and poetry. He studied philosophy with his famous teacher, Socrates. Plato founded a school for

philosophers and wrote some of the most famous stories and works of the ancient Greek age, including *The Republic* and *Apology*. He often wrote in dialogues— imagined conversations

Plato's teacher, Socrates

between different people. Plato died peacefully in bed at the age of about eighty.

No one knows if Plato's story of gods and demigods in Atlantis is true. Plato, after all, was a pretty creative thinker. And he was a great storyteller.

Parts of the Atlantis story are pretty clearly not true: the demigods and the god Zeus punishing the Atlanteans. People think that Plato may have made the story up to teach a lesson about what happens when people get too greedy.

But Plato's story is strangely detailed. He even includes the location of Atlantis—just west of the Strait of Gibraltar. The Strait of Gibraltar

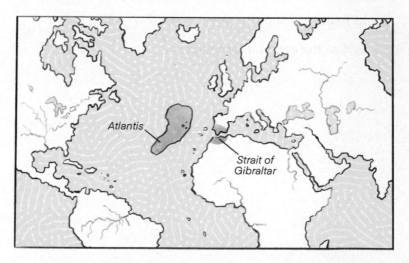

is the narrow strip of ocean that separates Spain and the northern coast of Africa. Plato notes exactly how big Atlantis was, with measurements. Why would he include all these details about a made-up city if he was just trying to teach a lesson?

Could Plato have used the history of a *real* city? A city that really *did* sink into the ocean, carrying all its treasures and beauty with it? Maybe Plato just exaggerated the story of that real city and added his own details about the gods.

Or maybe not. Explorers, researchers, and ordinary people have devoted their lives to finding out the truth. Where is Atlantis? What *was* Atlantis? Why did this city of gold and silver disappear so suddenly? And could we possibly find it again?

Since Plato's time, people have enjoyed the story of Atlantis so much that they've told and retold it. Even after Plato died, other ancient Greeks kept the story alive. Plutarch, another philosopher, reminded his readers of Plato's story five hundred years later.

Plutarch

Some took the story literally. A man named Crantor had been taught by a student of Plato's. He thought Atlantis had to be a real place and

traveled to Egypt to find proof that it existed. In Egypt, according to legend, Crantor found columns carved with hieroglyphs that spelled out the history of Atlantis.

Zoom forward a thousand or so years: The story of Atlantis had faded for most people. They'd moved on to other legends. But it wasn't completely forgotten. In 1492, Christopher Columbus sailed from Spain across the Atlantic

Ocean. As the *Niña*, the *Pinta*, and the *Santa Maria* neared land, Columbus was sure he had found the East Indies—what we now call India, China, and Japan. He also thought he just might be sailing near the location of Plato's Atlantis!

During the 1500s and 1600s, important and influential men like Thomas More (a British lawyer who served King Henry VIII) and Francis Bacon (attorney general and lord chancellor of England) wrote about Atlantis, too. They didn't spend their time sailing around looking for it, but they liked to think about perfect worlds and perfect people working perfectly together.

For Columbus, and other explorers and philosophers, Atlantis had been more of a dream than a reality. They wondered about it and wrote about it. They never seriously considered trying to find it. But a few hundred years later, all of that would change.

CHAPTER 2
Atlantis Explosion

In the mid-1800s, the United States and Europe went through a rapid change as society began to move from a mostly rural farming life to one filled with new inventions, fast-moving machinery, and factory work. Charles Darwin was writing about his new ideas about plants and animals. Thomas Edison would soon invent the electric lightbulb. People read about these discoveries with interest. And authors were exploring scientific themes as well. Some began to write a new

Charles Darwin

Thomas Edison

kind of story that combined scientific and technological advances with adventure. These stories are called science fiction. And some of them were about the beautiful, mysterious lost city of Atlantis.

Sometime around 1870, in Nininger City, Minnesota, a man named Ignatius Donnelly was reading a translation of a new science fiction story called *Twenty Thousand Leagues Under the Sea*, by the French author Jules Verne. Jules wrote of Captain Nemo, who takes Professor Aronnax on board his electric submarine and travels deep under the sea. On their adventures, they find the sunken ruins of a great city—and a black rock carved with the word "Atlantis."

Ignatius read on. He sat up and put his book down. He'd been having a difficult time recently. After his time in the Minnesota State Senate and several terms as a US congressman, he had left politics. He was all alone in his big house. He needed a project. Now the seeds of that project began to grow in his imagination.

Jules Verne (1828–1905)

Jules Verne grew up near the Loire River in France and often watched the ships coming and going along the waterfront. Throughout his life, Jules was interested in travel and adventure. His father wanted him to be a lawyer, but Jules liked to write plays and stories. He was working as a stockbroker when he got the idea to write a science fiction story.

In 1863, Jules published *Five Weeks in a Balloon*. The book was a hit, and Jules quit his job and started writing full-time. In addition to *Twenty Thousand Leagues Under the Sea*, Jules also wrote a book called *Around the World in Eighty Days*, about a man who tries to travel around the world on a bet. Jules's books were very popular. For the rest of his life, he would write and sail on his ship with his wife, Honorine. Jules died in 1905 at age seventy-seven.

Ignatius decided he was going to write a book about Atlantis. As he wrote, he started to feel better. His book, published in 1882, was called

Atlantis: The Antediluvian World. "Antediluvian" means before the time of Noah's flood in the Bible. But it can also mean "very, very old."

In the book, Ignatius had done something no one else had done before.

He didn't just wonder if Atlantis was real or not. He said it *was* real. (Not the parts about the gods Poseidon and Zeus or the demigods. But the rest of it.) Ignatius had decided that Plato's story was factually accurate!

But even more than that, Ignatius said, the Atlanteans had invented gunpowder, paper, and farming. When their city sank under the waves, Ignatius wrote, not all the Atlanteans died.

Some escaped. They paddled away in boats and went on to start other great civilizations. He felt that *other* great civilizations in the world had originated in Atlantis.

Ignatius Donnelly included what he called scientific evidence that Atlantis was real. He said that it was definitely in the middle of the Atlantic Ocean. He said that the Gulf Stream current flowed clockwise in the Atlantic Ocean because it was actually flowing around the sunken island of Atlantis! Ignatius knew that scientists had recently found mountains with volcanoes at the bottom of the ocean floor. In his book,

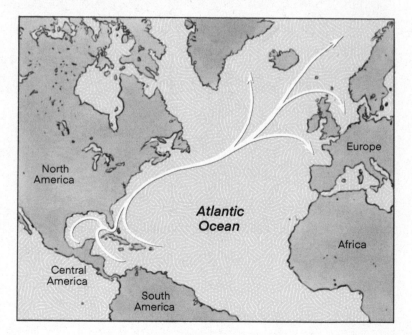

The Gulf Stream

he stated that at the bottom of the ocean was where the sunken island would be found.

Atlantis: The Antediluvian World became very popular. The prime minister of England sent Ignatius a note of congratulations. Charles Darwin read the book, though he questioned the science in it. Newspapers called it one of the notable books of the century. All of a sudden, Ignatius was famous, and the book was a best seller.

Everywhere, people once again became fascinated with the story of Atlantis. Some people believed what Ignatius had written in his book, but others took their Atlantis beliefs a little further. They began to develop theories about Atlantis that were related to the supernatural. A Russian psychic named Madame Blavatsky was an especially big Atlantis fan. She invented her own religion, called Theosophy, based on supernatural beliefs.

Madame Blavatsky

In 1888, to support her new religion, Madame Blavatsky wrote a series of books called *The Secret Doctrine*. She said that all humanity had come from different sources, including a kind of invisible jellyfish, other invisible beings that lived near the North Pole, lemurs with eyes in the back of their heads, humans, and—Atlanteans. The Atlanteans, Madame Blavatsky wrote, were superhumans who had electricity and traveled by airship.

Most people did not believe in Madame Blavatsky's theories, but many were starting to believe that Atlantis was real. More and more people were interested in finding scientific proof that Atlantis had existed. They wanted to find the lost city. After all, ruins of ancient civilizations had been discovered before. Why not Atlantis?

CHAPTER 3
Other Atlantises

Whole cities and civilizations can be wiped out by natural disasters. It has happened. In 79 CE, the Roman city of Pompeii was covered with lava when nearby Mount Vesuvius erupted. Clouds of ash and superheated air engulfed the city.

People were killed instantly as they slept in their beds, ate dinner, or visited with their neighbors. In hours, the entire city was wiped out.

Other civilizations came to an end more slowly and more mysteriously. Around 985 CE, Norse Vikings sailed to the vast, frozen continent of Greenland. They built turf-home settlements,

fished, and raised sheep and cattle for four hundred years. Then they slowly moved on from their colonies in Greenland. No one knows exactly why. The last Greenlandic settlers died or boarded boats off the island around 1400 CE, leaving their centuries-old homes to crumble and blow away in the subarctic wind.

These civilizations—and many others—seemed to disappear in various ways. And there are many ideas about what happened to Atlantis. According to Plato, Atlantis had disappeared in an earthquake or volcanic eruption, which caused the island to sink. Is that even possible?

Scientists say that it definitely is. There are a couple of ways it could happen. Both involve volcanoes. For the first, there might be a volcano on an island in the ocean, making little eruptions for a long time—millions of years.

Each time it erupts, ash and rock build up to form a cone shape. And under the cone, a huge pool of boiling hot liquid rock—called magma—forms. The magma is so hot that it melts a chamber—a big hollow place—in the earth.

Then, one day, with no warning whatsoever, the entire pool of magma in the chamber erupts. It explodes out of the volcano's cone. The volcano collapses into the empty magma chamber. It disappears down, down into the ground and leaves behind a huge hole. Ocean water fills up the hole. And whatever was on top of the ground is . . . gone.

The second way happens much more slowly. Scientists know that when Earth goes through a warming cycle, ice melts from glaciers. The melted ice pours into the sea and the sea rises higher and higher. Gradually, the sea creeps up and up, lapping at the edges of an island. Then, perhaps a volcano erupts on another,

nearby island. The massive explosion makes huge waves, called tsunamis. The tsunamis crash over the already sinking island and erode the rest of the land enough that the sea covers it.

So in the real world, there *could* have been a large island that suddenly sank under the sea, in the same way natural disasters have destroyed other cities and civilizations. Maybe Atlantis could have existed. Plato's story was, maybe, not just a story. If someone looked hard enough, could they find the sunken city that has captivated treasure hunters for more than a century? But where on earth could Atlantis be?

A Real-Life Atlantis Experience?

On December 22, 2018, the people living on the islands of Sumatra and Java in the country of Indonesia experienced what the Atlanteans might have experienced. The day was an ordinary one. Then, as darkness fell over the islands, they ate dinner with their families, watched a little TV, and got ready for bed.

But right around 9:30 p.m., a massive rumbling was heard outside. People rushed to their windows to see a huge wave of water crashing down over the islands. Water swept through the towns, flattening buildings. Over 14,000 people were seriously injured and 437 people died.

Sumatra and Java had just experienced a tsunami.

This tsunami was caused by the eruption of Anak Krakatau, a simmering, burbling volcano that

sat in the ocean off the coast of Indonesia. Anak Krakatau had been threatening to erupt for several months. When it did, huge chunks of it slid off into the ocean. The giant splashes caused oversize waves to travel across the open ocean and slam into the shores of the neighboring islands—destroying entire sections of the islands. This is a modern example of what might have happened to Atlantis many, many years ago.

CHAPTER 4
The Atlantis Requirements

Generations of archeologists, scientists, and other curious people have asked themselves the same question: How hard could finding Atlantis really be? After all, Plato provides specific details in his story. All an Atlantis hunter would have to do is list those details, find a place that matches them all, and boom! Atlantis found.

So, what *are* the details? A good Atlantis hunter knows that Atlantis was on an island and that this island was as big as a continent. Atlantis hunters would need to find evidence that wealthy, sophisticated people had once lived there. They'd have to find furniture, art, and carved stone— those things are in Plato's story. The people on this island needed to have known how to work with metal, because Plato says that precious metals decorated the Atlantean walls. And Atlantis hunters would need to find evidence of the kind of massive temple that Plato described.

But there's more. According to Plato, Atlantis had a huge system of concentric rings—alternating rings of both earth and water that lay one inside the other. Also, the island would need to have a flat plain for growing crops, and mountains. According to Plato's story, the people who lived in Athens, Greece, could reach Atlantis easily. So Atlantis would need to be within sailing distance of Athens. And Plato also said that Atlantis was near the Pillars of Hercules—stony mountains on each side of the Strait of Gibraltar (the strip of ocean between Spain and northern Africa).

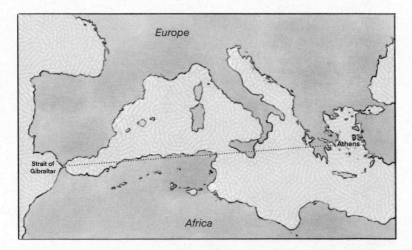

And Atlantis would have been destroyed by some kind of terrible natural disaster, around 9600 BCE.

For centuries, people thought that all someone would have to do to find Atlantis is locate one place on earth that had all the details Plato described.

Archeologists and other scientists looked both on dry land and on the bottom of the sea. They realized that Atlantis could have been swamped by a huge tsunami and covered with water, but if the water retreated, the city might be buried by earth and debris on an island.

The Pillars of Hercules

On both sides of where the Mediterranean Sea meets the Atlantic Ocean, massive natural rock pillars rise from the sloshing water. These rock formations lie just over eight and a half miles apart across a waterway known as the Strait of Gibraltar. Gibraltar, Spain, lies on one side and Jebel Musa, Morocco, on the other.

The northern pillar, called the Rock of Gibraltar, stands around 1,400 feet tall—about the height of Big Ben. There are actually two peaks located to the south—Jebel Musa, which is about 2,799 feet tall, and the smaller Mount Hacho, at about 700 feet tall.

The ancient Greek poets wrote stories of how the stone pillars came to exist. In one story, the demigod Hercules tore the continents of Europe and Africa apart, then lifted the pillars to mark what he had done. In another story, he pulled the continents together, with only a narrow passage between, raising the pillars from the ocean as a monument to himself.

The rock formation of **Jebel Musa, Morocco**

The rock formation of **Gibraltar, Spain**

If Atlantis is still lying on the bottom of the ocean floor, it would be covered with many layers of silt and sand. But with modern technology, Atlantis hunters might be able to peer down through the ocean waters to spot the remnants of the sunken city.

Finding the ruins of Atlantis might be possible, Atlantis hunters have concluded. But how to narrow down the search?

CHAPTER 5
Where in the World?

Deciding exactly where to begin the search for Atlantis is not that simple. Plato's guidelines could be interpreted to mean just about anything. There have been many educated guesses. And throughout history, people often declared they could prove that their guess was the right spot.

In the seventeenth century, a doctor and archeologist named Olaus Rudbeck became obsessed with Atlantis. He wrote a series of huge books about the city, called *Atlantica*. Olaus was convinced that the ruins of Atlantis were actually located in Sweden.

Olaus Rudbeck

In his archeology work, Olaus had been digging in a Swedish village called Old Uppsala. He was excavating burial mounds—mounds of earth created by ancient people to bury their dead. He uncovered some strange, very *tall* human skeletons. And Olaus decided that these were the skeletons of the ancient Atlanteans and that Old Uppsala must have been the capital of Atlantis.

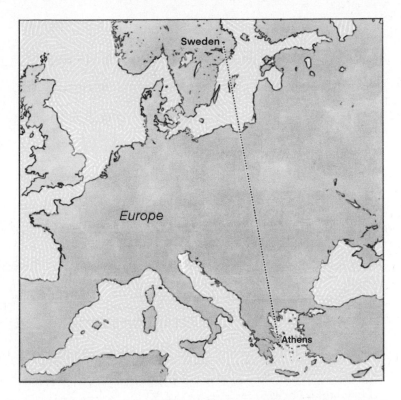

The country of Sweden is over two thousand miles from Athens, Greece. And Atlantis, according to Plato, was supposed to be easily reachable from Athens. So perhaps Olaus should have done more research. But he didn't think so. Olaus died in 1702, still utterly convinced that Atlantis was located in ancient Sweden.

Three hundred years later, in the 1970s, a writer named Charles Berlitz said that he thought Atlantis had been a continent off the coast of the Caribbean nation of Bermuda. Bermuda is a large island about six hundred miles off the eastern coast of the United States, and part of a mysterious section of ocean called the Bermuda Triangle.

Charles Berlitz

Charles Berlitz wrote that he believed Atlantis had sunk down into the Bermuda Triangle and was swallowed up by whatever mysterious force was at work in that area. People who have investigated Charles's theory even found strange formations under the ocean there. They looked like man-made walls and stone structures. But later, scientists determined that they were simply natural rock formations.

The Bermuda Triangle

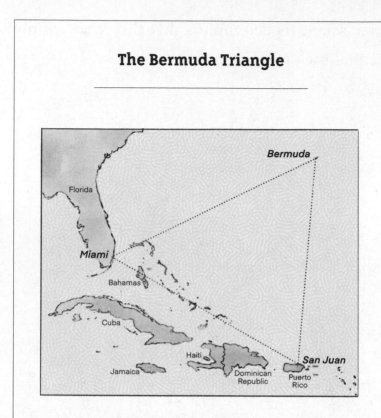

In 1945, five United States Navy bombers left their base in Florida and headed east over the Atlantic Ocean on a training run. Their planes disappeared without a trace. Then a rescue plane disappeared in the same spot. Were strange forces at work?

Since the beginning of the twentieth century, people have told stories about the section of ocean that has come to be known as the Bermuda Triangle. Planes and ships have mysteriously vanished over the triangle, an area of land stretching from the east coast of Florida to Bermuda to the Greater Antilles, a group of islands that includes Cuba and Puerto Rico.

Many hurricanes and tropical storms pass through the area of the Bermuda Triangle. These storms sank many ships in the days before modern weather forecasting. Scientists know that the Gulf Stream, a major ocean current, often causes weather to change quickly and violently. This can also cause ships to sink and planes to crash. But many of the vessels that have gone missing in the triangle have never been recovered. And so questions about the mysterious Bermuda Triangle remain unanswered.

Some people even believe that Atlantis is buried under the ice sheets of Antarctica, which is about nine thousand miles from Athens! People who believe Atlantis is there call their theory the Earth Crust Displacement theory. They believe that sometimes the outer crust of the earth suddenly shifts, shooting continents and other landforms swiftly around the globe. And they believe this is what happened to Atlantis.

Also, according to these thinkers, Antarctica wasn't always cold. Their theory is that in 9600 BCE, around the time Plato gives for the destruction of Atlantis, Antarctica was positively warm—tropical, in fact. Scientists say this is not true. Antarctica *was* tropical at one point in history but that was during the Cretaceous period, ninety million years ago!

Earth Crust Displacement theory states that when Plato described the earthquakes that destroyed Atlantis, he was *actually* describing the huge shocks of the earth's crust shifting. Fans of the theory believe that Atlantis, as a part of the continental crust, was suddenly and forcefully moved to Antarctica, which then froze over. The ruined city is now trapped under massive layers of ice. If scientists were

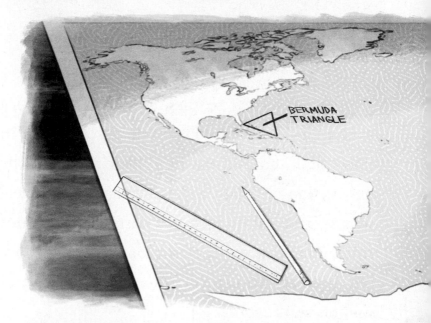

BERMUDA TRIANGLE

only able to explore the region under the ice sheets, they just might find the ruins of Atlantis. (Or so believe the Earth Crust Displacement theorists.)

Of course, no one can say for certain if Atlantis is in Sweden or Antarctica or at the bottom of the Bermuda Triangle, but there are other theories that Atlantis is somewhere closer to Athens and Plato's original geographic clues.

Where could Atlantis be?

CHAPTER 6
Closer to (Plato's) Home

The island of Malta, in the Mediterranean Sea, is a peaceful, sleepy place full of fancy old Italian buildings, yellow rocks, and sandy beaches. Some Atlantis hunters believe it is also one possible location of the lost city.

Temple ruins of Malta

Malta checks a lot of the boxes Plato laid out: It's near Athens, Greece. It's an island. It's full of old ruins from ancient civilizations, including temples, just as the Atlanteans were said to have built. Some of these temples are even older than those in Egypt. Many of the ruins near Malta are underwater now—just as the ruins of Atlantis might be. And the ancient people of Malta vanished long ago—but no one knows why.

Archeologists have even uncovered a system of grids carved into the stone that look strangely like the concentric trenches of water Plato described. Could this be *the* place?

But Malta does not have a mountain, which Plato definitely said Atlantis had. And it doesn't have a huge plain, which Plato also said Atlantis had. So perhaps Malta does not check *all* the boxes.

There may be a location that *does* have all the geography Plato described. The plain of Souss-Massa in Morocco matches every geographic detail of Plato's story. How do Atlantis hunters know this?

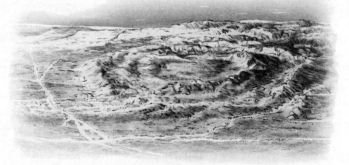

SOUSS-MASSA IN MOROCCO

In the 2000s, a computer programmer named Michael Hubner made a list of every detail about Atlantis's land and water characteristics that Plato mentioned. Then he plugged all fifty-one of them into a global mapping program to see which location would fit. He needed to find a location near the sea that was also

Michael Hubner

near the Pillars of Hercules and not in Europe or Asia, but was west of Egypt and had both mountains to the north and elephants, was shaped like a ring, and was within 3,100 miles of Athens. Plus forty-two other characteristics! Simple, right? The computer came up with only one location that fit: the Souss-Massa plain in Morocco. Atlantis found!

Except for a few small problems. Atlantis was supposed to have been an island, surrounded by water. The plain of Souss-Massa is . . . a plain. It's dry. Except for the coast, there is very little water. Also, no ruins have been discovered anywhere on the plain. Perhaps the ruins are buried underground . . . waiting to be found.

Another possible Atlantis location *does* have a lost city—a famous one. Scientists even know its name: Tartessos. Tartessos was on the coast of Spain, near what is now the city of Cadiz. It fits a lot of Plato's descriptions. The people of Tartessos were very wealthy, but their civilization mysteriously disappeared. Tartessos is located near water and just outside the Pillars of Hercules. The area has a lot of copper—and the inhabitants of Atlantis were said to have mined a lot of metal.

The area around Tartessos has seen a lot of earthquakes and tsunamis—good for wiping out cities. And photos taken by satellite have shown an area of large circles in the ground—just as Plato described.

Tartessos, however, has the same problems as Morocco and Malta—it has many of the features Plato described, but not all of them. The biggest problem? The coast of Spain near Tartessos is not an island. And there is no other island nearby. Plato did say that Atlantis was an island.

So if Atlantis isn't in Antarctica, Sweden, the Bermuda Triangle, Malta, Morocco, or off the coast of Spain, then did Atlantis *ever* exist outside of Plato's mind?

CHAPTER 7
Atlantis Found?

During the Bronze Age, from around 3300 BCE to 1200 BCE, people called Minoans lived on the island of Santorini, in what is now modern Greece. They were fabulously wealthy. Their capital city, Akrotiri, was filled with two- and three-story buildings, elaborate murals and frescoes,

Minoan fresco

and a huge palace that included a throne carved from a type of rock called gypsum. The Minoans had plenty of ships that they used to travel the world to trade with their allies. The island had plains for farming. Natural rock channels lay in concentric circles around the island, with a canal up the middle. Santorini also had a mountain. And that mountain was also an active volcano, also called Akrotiri.

Sometime around 1500 BCE, the volcano began to rumble and spit. It puffed out clouds of smoke and gas. The trembling grew stronger and stronger. Then, one day, clouds of ash billowed out, turning day into night, as poisonous gases and superheated air rolled over the land. The volcano collapsed, dragging the surrounding land down into the sea, as huge waves crashed over it. The Minoans were wiped out. They were gone. Their beautiful city was gone, too.

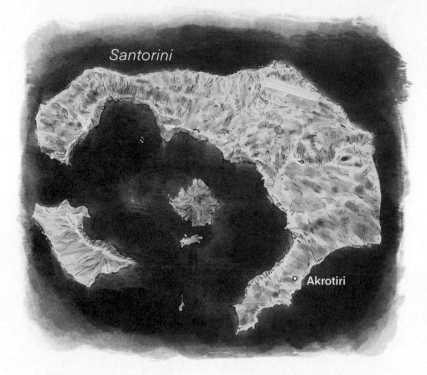

The sea settled. Santorini was now a huge sunken round crater, called a caldera. A bit of dry land still stuck up above the water. The ash from the volcano drifted down onto the land. It hardened. Time passed. Trees grew and animals returned. People returned, too. They built houses and farms. For over three thousand years, Akrotiri slept in peace.

Then, in the late nineteenth century, miners on the island began finding pieces of ancient artifacts as they worked. Over time, archeologists started to take a closer look and began unearthing buildings, art, urns, and even parts of cloth-weaving looms. By the time Spyridon Marinatos unearthed the city of Akrotiri in 1967, people were already guessing that this *might* be Atlantis, at long last.

A clay figurine unearthed on Santorini

There were still a few problems, though. Santorini isn't exactly "just outside" the Pillars of Hercules near the Strait of Gibraltar. It's actually seventeen hundred miles away, clear on the other side of North Africa. Also, Plato gave a lot of measurements for Atlantis. He said the plain where the Atlanteans grew crops measured two hundred miles by three hundred miles.

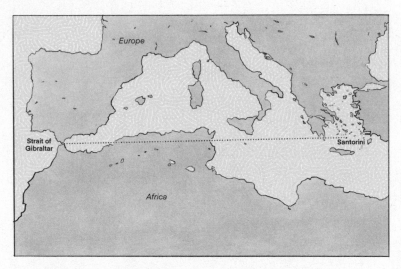

He said the canal the ships sailed through was a thousand miles long. And he said Atlantis had disappeared around 9600 BCE.

If these numbers were correct, and not just an exaggeration, then Atlantis couldn't have been on Santorini. The island is too small, even before the volcano exploded. And the explosion happened around 1500 BCE, eight thousand years after the year Plato gave for Atlantis's disappearance. A Greek scientist named Angelos Galanopoulos had a solution for these little problems. In the 1960s, he wrote that he believed there had been a mistake when Plato's story was being translated. Someone had accidentally substituted the symbol for one hundred with the symbol

Galanopoulos's book

for one thousand. All Plato's numbers and years were recorded as way bigger than had actually been written. Plato *meant* the plain was twenty miles by thirty miles. The canal was one hundred miles long, not one thousand. And Atlantis disappeared somewhere around 1500 to 1000 BCE—just at the time that the volcano on Santorini destroyed the Minoans.

As for the Pillars of Hercules and the Strait of Gibraltar problem, Angelos said not to worry. No one *really* knows what Plato meant by the "Pillars of Hercules." Perhaps he was referring

Hercules

to an entirely different rock formation—in an entirely different part of the world. Perhaps a part of the world near Greece. And Santorini.

Angelos really believed that Atlantis is on Santorini. Olaus Rudbeck thought Atlantis is in Sweden. And Charles Berlitz was positive that Atlantis is in the Bermuda Triangle. But each of these—everyone who has a favorite Atlantis location—has to twist the numbers, or ignore certain parts of Plato's story, or explain away the parts that don't fit. People *want* to find Atlantis and to know for certain that it existed. So they continue to try to make it true. They have woven it into art, books, music, and movies. The story of Atlantis gets told and told again because it continues to live in our imaginations, even though it has not yet been found.

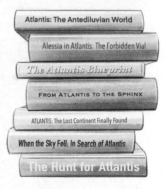

Atlantis: The Antediluvian World

Alessia in Atlantis: The Forbidden Vial

The Atlantis Blueprint

FROM ATLANTIS TO THE SPHINX

ATLANTIS: The Lost Continent Finally Found

When the Sky Fell: In Search of Atlantis

The Hunt for Atlantis

CHAPTER 8
On the Page

Whether it's true or not, the story of Atlantis is irresistible. It has been written into the lyrics of songs like "Atlantis Is Calling" by the group SOS for Love, "Voyage to Atlantis," by the Isley Brothers, "Shipwrecked in Atlantis," by Busted, and "Searching for Atlantis," by the group Saxon. In the movie *Hotel Transylvania 3*, the characters

cruise to Atlantis on a ship called *Legacy* in search of a magic device. In *Aquaman*, the superhero is half-human, half-Atlantean. The characters in the Disney film *Atlantis: The Lost Empire* find directions to Atlantis and drive a submarine to the Lost City.

Entire TV series have been dedicated to the lost city, like *Atlantis*, which ran from 2013 to 2015. In this version of the Atlantis story, the main character drives a submarine to the bottom of the ocean, falls asleep, and wakes up in the Lost City.

People can actually experience Atlantis—in the form of a massive resort and waterpark in the Bahamas called . . . Atlantis. Towering buildings are supposed to look as if they've risen straight out of the sea. Palm trees, waterfalls, and pools are meant to make visitors feel as if they're actually in paradise. The builder Sol Kerzner wanted to re-create the Atlantis myth—except with the modern additions of a waterpark and a nightclub.

The world of comic books has always been a place of imaginative and amazing other universes. And the story of Atlantis has been woven into comics since their earliest days. In 1949, a comic book called *The Sub-Mariner* featured a story about the underwater city, which is ruled by a half human, half sea creature named Namor, the Sub-Mariner. Namor and his magical kingdom appeared in over 4,500 Marvel comics over the years. Atlanteans lived under glass domes they had built under the sea, so they could survive. They fought their enemies in the settlement of Mu, and traveled to found other settlements. Namor became Prince Namor and even fought against the Nazis during World War II.

SpongeBob Visits Atlantis

Since 1999, when the show was first broadcast, the little yellow ocean-loving sponge, SpongeBob SquarePants, has visited the moon, the desert, a bomb-testing facility, Toys "R" Us, the Mariana Trench (the deepest point of the ocean), and infinity. SpongeBob finally visited Atlantis, too, in 2007's Season 5, episode 12: "Atlantis SquarePantis."

In the episode, Spongebob finds half of an ancient medallion and reconnects it with its other half at a museum. Suddenly, a van appears and takes Spongebob and his friends straight to Atlantis. They meet the Atlantean king, Lord Royal Highness, who was voiced by rock legend David Bowie. Lord Royal Highness gives them a tour of Atlantis, and each character sees what they are most excited about—culture, gold and jewels, advanced technology—and for SpongeBob, a treasure called the Oldest Living Bubble. It seems that, even in SpongeBob's world, Atlantis can become whatever a person wishes it to be.

In the DC comics world, Atlantis first appeared in *Adventure Comics* in 1959. In this universe, Atlantis is ruled by Aquaman, the son of a lighthouse keeper and an Atlantean princess. As King of Atlantis, Aquaman lords over a realm divided into city-states—each located on a different continent on Earth. The magical, mystical Atlanteans eventually leave Earth to explore the rest of the universe.

Atlantis even showed up in the Disney comic world when, in the 1954 comic *The Sunken City*, grumpy Scrooge McDuck journeys to the bottom of the sea to fetch a single quarter. Down there in the depths, he finds . . . Atlantis! This time Atlantis is filled with mutants called Water People, who get their electricity from electric eels. They keep Atlantis hidden under a layer of glowing fish bones.

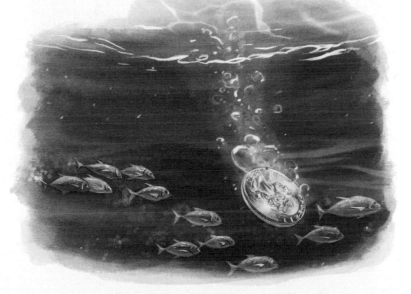

Scrooge eventually gets his quarter back and returns to the surface. The comic book world of Atlantis is left glowing at the bottom of the ocean. And this is one of the reasons the story of Atlantis is so appealing: Writers and artists can make it whatever they want it to be.

That's what the best stories do. Maybe this is why the story of Atlantis has survived for thousands of years.

CHAPTER 9
Imagining Atlantis

No one knows what Plato intended when he wrote the story of Atlantis. He had heard stories of exploding mountains and enormous waves. He knew about the destruction that erupting volcanoes could cause.

Many people throughout history believed that Plato took real geological events— an erupting volcano, the destruction of an island, massive ocean waves—and wove them into a story of beauty, greed, power,

and loss. Scientists call this type of storytelling "geomythology."

Other storytellers around the world have done this, too. In the Solomon Islands nation, near Papua New Guinea, islanders have long told the story of a man who bought a curse to punish his wife. The curse sent eight massive waves crashing onto the island of Teonimanu, where the man's wife was living, sinking it into the ocean.

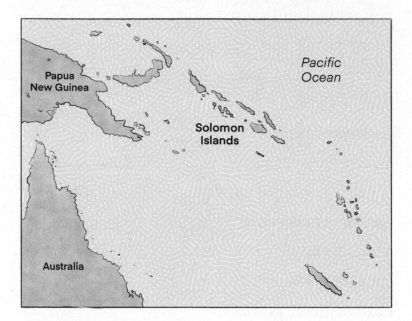

Now scientists working there believe that this myth is based on a real geological event. Several hundred years ago, an earthquake in the sea destroyed part of the underwater ridge that supported the island. A landslide carried Teonimanu under the water, and this land movement created a train of tsunamis.

An ancient Indian book called *The Mahabharata* tells another story, about the long-ago city of Dwarka, in the region of Gujarat, on the western coast of India. Dwarka was a beautiful place built by the god Krishna himself, who raised the city directly from the sea, then surrounded it with a stone wall to protect it. The people of Dwarka lived in gorgeous houses, surrounded by wealth. But when Lord Krishna left to live in heaven, the city sank into the Arabian Sea and was lost.

Lord Krishna

In 1963, scientists found ruins of a city off the coast of Gujarat. By 1990, they had confirmed the ruins were those of Dwarka, under the water. It was a real place. Scientists believe that people were watching the sea levels rise and the waves lap closer and closer to their homes in cities on the coast. A tsunami similar to the one that hit India in 2004 may also have submerged the city.

Imagine, though, a *reverse* Atlantis—an island rising from the sea where none had been before. This is what happened before the eyes of astonished fishermen off the coast of Sicily in July 1831. After powerful sulfur gas rose from the ocean waters, a volcano slowly emerged above the surface. It grew and grew until it was a rock island

L'Isola che se ne andò

about half a mile wide. No one knew what to think. Quickly, France and the United Kingdom started fighting Sicily for ownership of the new island. But within five months, the island sank back beneath the waves. People called it "L'isola che se ne andò"—The Island That Went Away.

A Different Kind of Lost City

In 2019, a group of scientists found a beautiful and strange collection of hot-water vents in an underwater mountain chain in the middle of the Atlantic Ocean, midway between North America and northern Africa. These hydrothermal vents are cracks on the seafloor that allow heated water to pour out. They are commonly found near volcanically active regions.

The scientists took a research vessel called the *Atlantis* to explore the vents, which sit on top of a huge underwater mountain they called "Atlantis"— their Lost City. And even though the vents look like towering buildings clustered together deep underwater, they are actually rock chimneys bubbling with superheated water from deep under the ground.

Research vessel *Atlantis*

Scientists have studied the area around Sicily and know that it is full of volcanic and earthquake activity. It's no wonder the island emerged, then sank.

Atlantis fascination still grips people around the world. In the last decade, some have come to believe that the Italian island of Sardinia might in fact be the actual site of Atlantis. Even though it is about 850 miles from the Strait of Gibraltar, supporters of this idea think that the Pillars of Hercules actually refers to the strait between Sicily and Tunisia—were Sardinia lies. Archeological digs on the island have uncovered gold, silver, and crystal jewelry, lamps, metal tools, and bronze figurines. Carefully built stone towers dot the land. But the civilization

Sardinian bronze figurine

that created these things disappeared. Scientists now believe that a meteorite may have hit the ocean near Sardinia, causing a massive wave to overwhelm the island. Atlantis? Or not?

Meanwhile, the archeological dig of Akrotiri on Santorini continues and is now protected by a new, climate-control roof. Walkways weave throughout the ruins so visitors can see the artifacts up close. And as scientists continue to dig, they find more and more delicate urns and vessels and colorful, elaborate frescoes that show a leisurely, wealthy life. In 2020, archeologists uncovered exquisite shell-shaped pottery, parts of necklaces, and double-edged bronze axes. This really could be it, some archeologists say. Akrotiri really *could* be Atlantis.

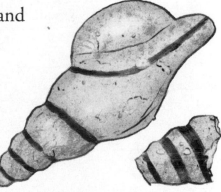

Shell-shaped pottery found in Akrotiri

Still, no one has proved this. While the cities and treasures found on Sardinia or Santorini or Malta and in Spain are as real as New York or Paris or Nairobi are today, we still haven't found the glowing city on the island just outside the Pillars of Hercules. It seems as if Atlantis exists—for now—only in our imaginations.

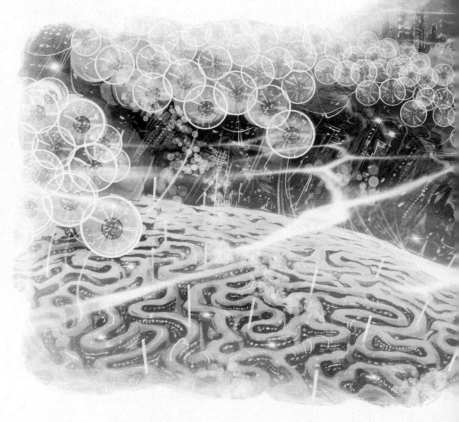

Timeline of Atlantis

9600 BCE —	Atlantis destroyed, according to Plato
1500 BCE —	Volcano on the Greek island of Santorini erupts, partly destroying the island
360 BCE —	Plato writes about Atlantis in *Timaeus and Critias*
1627 —	Philosopher Francis Bacon's novel, *The New Atlantis*, is published
1702 —	Olaus Rudbeck writes *Atlantica*, claiming Atlantis was in ancient Sweden
1867 —	Archeological excavations on Santorini begin
1870 —	Jules Verne writes *Twenty Thousand Leagues Under the Sea*
1882 —	Ignatius Donnelly publishes *Atlantis: The Antediluvian World*
1949 —	Atlantis is first featured in the Marvel *Sub-Mariner* comic book
1959 —	Atlantis is first featured in DC *Adventure Comics*
1967 —	Archeologist Spyridon Marinatos unearths the ancient city of Akrotiri on Santorini
1974 —	Charles Berlitz speculates that Atlantis is in the Bermuda Triangle
2018 —	Scientists investigate underwater thermal chimneys they call "The Lost City"

Timeline of the World

10,000 BCE —	Humans begin to practice agriculture in what is now the Middle East
776 BCE —	The first Olympic Games are held in Athens, Greece
432 BCE —	The Parthenon temple is completed in Athens
1558 —	Elizabeth I becomes Queen of England
1610 —	Galileo proves that Earth and other planets revolve around the sun
1632 —	Mughal emperor Shah Jahan begins to build the Taj Mahal
1775 —	The American Revolution begins
1887 —	In Paris, France, construction starts on the Eiffel Tower
1968 —	Martin Luther King Jr. is assassinated in Memphis, Tennessee
1972 —	Five burglars break into the Democratic National Committee headquarters at the Watergate building
1990 —	The Hubble Space Telescope is launched into orbit around Earth
2013 —	Black Lives Matter protests begin in July in the United States after the acquittal of George Zimmerman in the shooting death of Trayvon Martin

Bibliography

*Books for young readers

Adams, Mark. *Meet Me in Atlantis: My Obsessive Quest to Find the Sunken City*. New York: Dutton, 2015.

Claus, Patricia. "New Findings on Santorini Point to 'Lost City of Atlantis' Origins." Greekreporter.com, May 21, 2021. https://greekreporter.com/2021/05/21/new-findings-on-santorini-point-to-lost-island-of-atlantis-origins/.

Derbyshire, John. "Jules Verne: Father of Science Fiction?" *The New Atlantis*, Spring 2006. https://www.thenewatlantis.com/publications/jules-verne-father-of-science-fiction.

*Donkin, Andrew. *Atlantis: The Lost City*. New York: DK, 2000.

Donnelly, Ignatius. *Atlantis: The Antediluvian World*, New York: Gramercy Publishing Company, 1964.

"Dwarka." *UNESCO Silk Roads Programme*, accessed September 14, 2021. https://en.unesco.org/silkroad/silk-road-themes/underwater-heritage/dwarka.

Giller, Geoffrey. "Where Is the Lost City of Atlantis—and Does It Even Exist?" *Discover*, July 21, 2020. https://www.discovermagazine.com/planet-earth/where-is-the-lost-city-of-atlantis-and-does-it-even-exist.

*Jazynka, Kitson. *History's Mysteries: Curious Clues, Cold Cases,*

and Puzzles from the Past. Washington, DC: National
Geographic, 2018.

Nunn, Patrick. "Vanished Islands and Hidden Continents of the
Pacific." PatrickNunn.org, accessed September 13, 2021.
https://patricknunn.org/writing/books/vanished-islands-
and-hidden-continents-of-the-pacific/.

Palmer, Jane. "The Atlantis-Style Myths That Turned Out to Be
True." *BBC.com*, January 19, 2016. http://www.tjanepalmer.
com/wp-content/uploads/2021/10/BBC-Earth-The-Atlantis-
style-myths-that-turned-out-to-be-true.pdf.

Pellegrino, Charles. *Unearthing Atlantis: An Archaeological
Odyssey*. New York: Random House, 1991.

"Spyridon Marinatos and the Discovery of Akrotiri." *SciHi Blog*,
November 4, 2020. http://scihi.org/spyridon-marinatos-
akrotiri/.

WHOHQ

YOUR HEADQUARTERS FOR HISTORY

Activities, Mad Libs, and sidesplitting jokes!
Discover the Who HQ books beyond the biographies